This book belongs to:

_____

All Kinds Of
FLOWER
RHYMES

Angela T. Hellman

PALMETTO
PUBLISHING
Charleston, SC
www.PalmettoPublishing.com

Copyright © 2024 by Angela T. Hellman

All rights reserved

No portion of this book may be reproduced, stored in a retrieval system, or transmitted in any form by any means—electronic, mechanical, photocopy, recording, or other—except for brief quotations in printed reviews, without prior permission of the author.

Hardcover ISBN: 9798822959323
Paperback ISBN: 9798822959330

To my mom whose contagious love for books and reading filled my childhood with many warm, cherished memories.

An amaryllis makes a great gift.

Petunias spread color bright and swift.

You'll spot daffodils
early in spring.

Pluck daisy petals
if love will ring.

Look at the lily dressed up so well.

Gardenias! Aaah, what a lovely smell.

The gorgeous orchid,

a true work of art.

Zinnias draw butterflies all around.

Foxgloves are bell-shaped
but don't make a sound.

Geraniums like living in pots.

Why are these flowers forget-me-nots?

God formed them all;

there's lots more to know.

Plant some of your own

to witness them grow.

Simple instructional drawing pages
that go along with flowers in this book
can be found on my website:
AngelaTHellmanbooks.com/author-website

Your voice truly matters. So if you enjoyed this book, please take a minute to leave a review on Amazon. Your kind feedback is important and so appreciated.

Many thanks,
Angela

Milton Keynes UK
Ingram Content Group UK Ltd.
UKHW051913291024
450402UK00005B/60